# Cooking It Up!

# COOKING IT UP!
## Recipes
### FROM THE BE STRONG AFTER SCHOOL CLUB

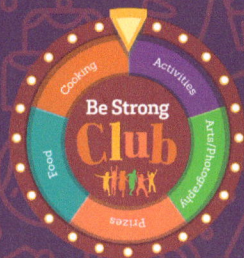

**Be Strong Club**

Cooking · Activities · Art/Photography · Prizes · Food

all write
publishing

Atlanta, GA

**Cooking It Up: Recipes from the Be Strong After School Club**

To request permissions, contact the publisher at info@allwritepublishing.com

Allwrite Publishing
P.O. Box 1071
Atlanta, GA 30301

www.AllwritePublishing.com

ISBN: 978-1-941716-07-6 (Hardback)

ISBN: 978-1-941716-08-3 (Paperback)

Library of Congress Control Number: 2021942081

Compiled by Vanessa Garcia, Jasmine Jean, Vasti Thomas, and the Be Strong After School Club

Cover design by Joey Q. Shephard

Layout by Joey Q. Shephard

Photographs by James Garcia, Be Strong After School Students and Staff

Printed in the USA

First print July 2021

## BREAKFAST

## APPETIZERS & ENTREES

## VEGGIE DISHES

## PASTA DISHES

## DESSERTS & DRINKS

# BE STRONG AFTER SCHOOL CLUB
## ACKNOWLEDGMENTS

Be Strong International, Inc. would like to acknowledge all of the funders of the Be Strong After School Club. It is through our funder's continuous financial support that middle school youth throughout Miami-Dade County are able to participate in our services FREE of cost.

This recipe book was paid for with funding provided by The Children's Trust, which primarily funds the Be Strong After School Club. The Children's Trust is a dedicated source of revenue established by voter referendum to improve the lives of children and families in Miami-Dade County.

Be Strong International is a 501(c)(3) non-profit organization, approved by the Internal Revenue Service as a tax-exempt, charitable organization. Donations collected on behalf of this recipe book will be used by Be Strong International, Inc. to continue providing holistic educational services and resources to youth and parents in broken families in order to help develop and maintain healthy relationships and thriving communities.

# BE STRONG
## INTERNATIONAL, INC.

**Healthy Relationships. Thriving Families. Stronger Communities.**

**MICHELLE SHIRLEY, CEO**

*Michelle has led the Be Strong International team since 2012.*

Be Strong
INTERNATIONAL

**B**e Strong International provides holistic educational services and resources to youth and parents from broken families in order for them to develop and maintain healthy relationships. For nearly 30 years, we have provided youth and parents in South Florida with tools to make better decisions about their personal, professional and social relationships, which can lead to a more promising future for themselves and the communities in which they reside.

The essence of our organization is "relationship." More specifically, we focus on how people relate to each other within personal and/or social associations. This is the heart of our organization and the basis of our relationship principles are centered around:

**Approach: Holistic** – we look at all aspects (heart, mind, body, spirit) of human beings and how they impact people's actions in relation to themselves and others.

**Skills: Healthy** – we use the latest research on human behavior and interactions to ensure that people understand and achieve more positive, healthy relationships.

**Outcome: Hopeful** – we ultimately want to provide a sense that there is hope for any relationship wherein all parties are committed to the same outcome.

## BE STRONG AFTER SCHOOL CLUB

The Be Strong After School Club is a unique enrichment program sponsored by The Children's Trust that guides the social, emotional and academic development of middle school youth, empowering them to be socially, physically, emotionally, and mentally healthy.

> **"**
>
> I love working with the Be Strong After School Club because it gives me an opportunity to share with our youth what I wish I could have learned when I was younger. The program allows me to teach life through the culinary world and impact our youth one meal at a time.
>
> **—Chef Vanessa a.k.a. "Chef V"**
> Chef & Owner of Picameal
>
> **"**

# CHEF VANESSA AND PICAMEAL

Vanessa & James Garcia, the founders of Picameal, had crossed paths to fulfill a vision with purpose. Building the company from the ground up, they have been modifying the catering industry with a unique style of what they now call "New Age Catering." One of the greatest issues in today's generation is that we are leaving dining tables desolated, their sole purpose being home decor. This society is causing humanity to be dissociated, and the result being, what use to be known as a "family home" has become just a living space.

Our main focus as a catering company is to rediscover family, friends, and homemade food with a twist of modernity. We like to bring unimaginable catering experiences from our kitchen to your special event. The menu is created with intentions to transport your guest back to a time of unity, indulging the heart in simple pleasures. Your event dishes are made fresh with a familiar homemade taste and the essential ingredients love & care, just like Mama would make.

# BREAKFAST

# GRINCH PANCAKES

**Made with love by Chef V**

## INGREDIENTS

### For Cream Cheese Icing Glaze

- 4 ounces cream cheese
- 1/2 cup powdered sugar
- 1 teaspoon pure vanilla extract
- 3-5 tablespoons milk

### For Green Whipped Cream

- 1/2 cup heavy whipping cream
- 2 tablespoons powdered sugar, sifted
- 1/2 teaspoon vanilla extract
- Green food coloring

### For Green Pancakes

- 1 1/4 cups all-purpose flour
- 1/8 teaspoon salt
- 1 teaspoon baking powder
- 1 teaspoon baking soda
- 1 egg, beaten
- 1 1/4 cups buttermilk
- 1/4 cup granulated sugar
- 2 tablespoons butter, melted
- 1 teaspoon pure vanilla extract
- Green food coloring
- Red heart candies or sprinkles

## INSTRUCTIONS

### For Cream Cheese Icing Glaze

Beat together the cream cheese, powdered sugar, vanilla and 3 tablespoons milk until smooth and creamy, adding more milk as needed until the icing is the desired consistency.

Set aside until needed.

### For Green Whipped Cream

Pour heavy whipping cream, sifted powdered sugar, vanilla, and a few drops of green food coloring into a mixing bowl.

Beat on low speed using an electric mixer until bubbles form. Then increase the speed to high and beat until the whipped cream holds stiff peaks.

Keep whipped cream refrigerated until needed up to 1 hour.

### Preparation

In large bowl, whisk the flour, salt, baking powder, and baking soda.

Whisk together the egg and buttermilk.

Pour into the flour mixture and stir to combine. Add sugar, melted butter, vanilla and green food coloring and mix until blended but with lumps remaining.

Drop a small amount of vegetable oil into a skillet or on a griddle and place over medium heat.

Once the oil begins to separate and move around the pan, use a paper towel to rub it into the pan, leaving just a light coating on the pan.

Ladle out about 1/4 cup of the green pancake batter onto the pan. Cook until bubbles begin to form on surface and edges begin to set.

Gently flip your pancakes over and cook until lightly browned on both sides.

Repeat with remaining batter making between 8 and 10 pancakes.

Stack warm pancakes on a plate and then spread on some of the cream cheese icing and add a dollop or swirl of green whipped cream.

Sprinkle on some candy hearts and serve immediately.

# TAYLORED PANCAKES

**Made with love by Vernon, age 13**

## INGREDIENTS

- Bisquick Shake 'n Pour Buttermilk
- Butter
- 1/8 teaspoon of salt
- Pepper
- 1 large egg
- Sausage (bacon or any protein of your choice)
- Aunt Jemima Syrup (or any syrup of your choice)

## INSTRUCTIONS

### For Eggs

Grease a pan and place on medium-high heat. Then immediately pour cracked egg inside pan.

Scramble your egg by stirring it until it is fully cooked. Then place your cooked egg to the side for later.

### For Sausage

Grease a pan and place it on medium-high heat. Then place sausage pieces inside the pan and fry it until fully cooked.

Then place cooked sausage to the side for later use.

## Preparation

Preheat a good quality, nonstick pan or griddle on medium heat first. Once it's hot, lower the heat down to low-medium heat.

Lightly grease the pan with a small amount of butter (yes, even on nonstick pans).

Pour a 1/4 cup of Bisquick Shake 'n Pour Buttermilk batter (or batter of your choice) so you get perfect, even-sized pancakes.

Start pouring the pancake batter into the middle of your heated pan, then continue pouring the batter slowly in a circular motion so that it spreads into perfect round shapes.

While one side of pancake is cooking, place your cooked eggs on one side and cooked sausage on the other side (or eggs and sausage can be mixed together, if preferred).

When the underside is golden and bubbles begin to appear on the surface, flip the pancake with a spatula and cook the other side until golden.

Remove from pan and serve on a plate, topping with syrup as desired.

### Be Strong After School Club Secret:

Vernon Taylor has been part of Be Strong After School Club for two years. Vernon expressed that he does not cook often; however, breakfast is his favorite meal of the day. He mentioned pancakes, sausage and eggs are his favorite. Ms. V suggested putting them all together so they could be tailored to all Vernon Taylor's favorites.

# CHEESY EXPLOSION PANCAKES

**Made with love by Genesis, age 14**

## INGREDIENTS

- 3 medium-sized potatoes
- Sugar
- Cornstarch
- Jack cheese
- Olive oil
- Salt

## INSTRUCTIONS

Remove the skin from the three potatoes.

Chop up the potatoes into smaller pieces and boil in salt water.

Smash the potatoes pieces in a pot. Then add sugar and cornstarch, while mixing and mashing at the same time until doughy consistency.

Shape the potato mixture into a pancake shape, adding your desired amount of jack cheese inside.

Place olive oil in the frying pan at medium-high heat. Immediately, add your potato pancake into the pan and cook until golden brown on both sides.

Remove from oil and serve.

# APPETIZERS & ENTREES

# PHILLY CHEESE STEAK SLIDERS

**Made with love by Chef V**

## INGREDIENTS

- 1 (12 ounce) beef skirt steak, thinly sliced
- 1 (12 count) package Hawaiian bread rolls
- 1/2 large green bell pepper, chopped
- 1/2 large onion, chopped
- 1/4 cup mayonnaise
- 8 slices Pepper Jack cheese
- 2 tablespoons butter, melted

## INSTRUCTIONS

Heat a skillet over medium-high heat. Add steak, bell pepper, and onion. Cook until steak is hot and reaches your desired color, 7 to 10 minutes.

Preheat the oven to 375 degrees F (190 degrees C). Line an 8x8-inch baking pan with aluminum foil.

Separate the rolls and then slice them in half to look like the top and bottom of a hamburger bun. Place the bottom half onto the bottom of the prepared baking pan. Spread mayonnaise evenly on top.

Place 4 slices of Pepper Jack cheese over the mayonnaise. Layer the steak mixture and the remaining cheese on top. Cover with the top half of the bread. Spread melted butter on top.

Bake in the preheated oven until cheese is melted and bread is browned, about 20 minutes. Slice into individual portions.

# CRUNCH WRAP SUPREME

**Made with love by Chef V**

## INGREDIENTS

- 2 tablespoons olive oil, divided
- 1 pound ground beef
- 1 package taco seasoning
- (4) 12-inch flour tortillas
- 1/2 cup nacho cheese
- 4 tostada shells
- 1/2 cup sour cream
- 2 cups shredded lettuce
- 1 tomato, diced
- 1 cup shredded Mexican blend cheese

## INSTRUCTIONS

Heat 1 tablespoon olive oil in a large skillet over medium high heat. Add ground beef and cook until beef has browned, about 3-5 minutes, making sure to crumble the beef as it cooks; stir in taco seasoning.

Drain excess fat; set aside.

Working one at a time, place ground beef mixture in the center of each tortilla. Top with nacho cheese and tostada shell. Spread sour cream in an even layer over the tostada shell; top with lettuce, tomato and cheese. Repeat with remaining tortillas.

Fold the edges up and over the center. Continue to work your way around the tortilla, folding as tight as possible.

Heat remaining 1 tablespoon olive oil in a large skillet. Place wrap seam-side down and cook until the underside is golden brown, about 2 minutes. Flip and cook wrap on the other side, about 1-2 minutes longer.

Serve immediately.

# TERIYAKI CHICKEN QUESADILLAS

**Made with love by Ms. Jasmine**

## INGREDIENTS

- 5 chicken breast tenderloins
- Cilantro (4 pieces)
- 1/2 Lemon (for juicing)
- Thyme (1 Teaspoon)
- Onion powder
- Garlic powder
- Garlic (4 chopped cloves)
- 1/8 of a scotch bonnet pepper (*optional if you like hot food)
- Sweet Baby Ray's Honey Teriyaki Sauce & Marinade
- Salt
- Pepper
- Non-Stick Oil Spray (or oil)

### Additional Topping (as pictured)

- Shredded cheddar cheese
- Chopped lettuce
- Diced tomatoes
- Diced onion

## INSTRUCTIONS

Preheat oven to 350 degrees.

Take a baking pan and spray it with non-stick oil spray. Then place the 5 chicken breast tenderloins inside of the baking pan.

On one side, season the chicken using 1/2 teaspoon of thyme, onion powder, and garlic powder. Flip the chicken breast and repeat the same seasonings on the other side.

Lightly pour Sweet Baby Ray's Honey Teriyaki Sauce & Marinade over the top of the chicken breast (only complete this on one side of the chicken breast).

Sprinkle the chopped garlic, chopped cilantro and chopped scotch bonnet pepper on top of the chicken.

Squeeze the juice from the 1/2 of lemon into the pan, not over the chicken so you do not wash off seasoning.

Bake the chicken in the oven for 25 minutes. Then remove chicken from the oven and cut it into pieces (see image above).

## INSTRUCTIONS (CONTINUED)

Add cut pieces of chicken back to pan and stir it in the remaining liquid.

Bake chicken in the oven for an additional 15 minutes before removing it.

### Additional Topping (as pictured)

Warm both sides of your tortillas on a skillet.

Add a scoop of the baked teriyaki chicken, diced onions, diced tomatoes, and chopped lettuce on one side of the tortilla. Then fold the other side of the tortilla over the toppings.

Allow it to cook for about 1 minute, and flip over to the other side to cook for another minute.

Once done, remove the quesadilla and add sour cream and cilantro to your taste.

Can make about 6 quesadillas depending on the amount of chicken used per tortilla.

# CILANTRO-LIME SHRIMP TACOS

Made with love by Chef V

## INGREDIENTS

- 2 tablespoons of freshly chopped cilantro
- 2 garlic cloves, crushed
- 1/2 teaspoon of cumin
- 1 tablespoon of olive oil
- Zest of 1 lime
- Kosher salt
- 1- lb. (pound) shrimp, peeled and deveined
- 8 tortillas, warmed, for serving

### For Cabbage Slaw

- 1 cup of shredded green cabbage
- 1/4 a cup of cilantro
- 1/4 red onion, thinly sliced
- 1/2 avocado, thinly sliced
- Juice of 1 lime
- 1 tablespoon of extra-virgin olive oil
- Kosher salt

### For Garlic-Lime Mayo

- 1/3 a cup of mayo
- 2 tablespoons of hot sauce
- Zest of 1 lime
- 1/2 teaspoon of garlic powder
- Kosher salt

## INSTRUCTIONS

In a large bowl, whisk together lime juice, cilantro, garlic, cumin, olive oil, lime zest and season with salt. Add shrimp and let marinate 20 minutes in refrigerator.

Then preheat grill or grill pan to medium heat. Grill shrimp until pink and white about 2 to 3 minutes per side.

### For Cabbage Slaw

In a large bowl combine all ingredients "For Cabbage Slaw." Toss gently to combine and season with salt.

### For Garlic-Lime Mayo

In a medium bowl, combine all ingredients "For Garlic-Lime Mayo." Whisk and season with salt.

### Preparation

Add a scoop of slaw, a few shrimp, and a drizzle of the garlic-lime mayo to each taco. Garnish with cilantro and serve.

# SHRIMP BAKED POTATO

**Made with love by Joi, age 13**

## INGREDIENTS

- 1 large potato
- Red pepper slices
- Green pepper slices
- Onion slices
- Peeled and deveined shrimp
- Mushrooms
- Salt
- Pepper
- Garlic
- Butter
- Sour cream (optional)

## INSTRUCTIONS

### For Baked Potato

Baked potatoes can be cooked many ways.

- Air fryer: Slice the potato down the middle and cook on 345 degrees for about 10 minutes or until soft.
- Oven: Put the potato in the oven for about 1 hour or until soft.
- Microwave: Poke holes in the potato with a fork and microwave on high for 10 minutes or until soft.

### For Shrimp

Add butter to a pan at medium-high heat.

Add and sauué peppers, onion, and mushrooms until they start to tender and brown.

Add shrimp into pan, while adding salt, pepper and garlic to your taste.

Cook for 10 minutes or until ready.
**Note:** Undercooked shrimp may be pink in color.

### Preparation

Cut your baked potato in half. Then place your shrimp, peppers, onions, and mushrooms on top of the baked potato halves.

Add butter, sour cream, cheese, or other toppings to your liking.

# FLAMIN' HOT CHICKEN TENDERS

**Made with love by Tiffany, age 14 (right) & Angie, age 14 (below)**

## INGREDIENTS

- 3 boneless skinless chicken tenderloins
- Kosher salt
- Freshly ground black pepper
- 1/3 cup of all-purpose flour
- 2 eggs, whisked with 1 tbsp. water
- 1 (9-oz.) bag of Flamin' Hot Cheetos, crushed
- Ranch dressing, for serving

## INSTRUCTIONS

Preheat oven to 400° and line a medium baking sheet with parchment paper.

Season chicken tenders generously with salt and pepper, then dredge in flour.

Next, dip tenders in egg, and then in Cheetos crumbs.

Place chicken on baking sheet and bake 25 minutes. Serve hot, with ranch dressing for dipping.

# FLAMIN' HOT MOZZARELLA STICKS

**Made with love by Chef V**

## INGREDIENTS

- Mozzarella Sticks
- Kosher salt
- Freshly ground black pepper
- 1/3 cup of all-purpose flour
- 2 eggs, whisked with 1 tbsp. water
- 1 (9-oz.) bag of Flamin' Hot Cheetos, crushed
- Ranch dressing, for serving

## INSTRUCTIONS

Preheat oven to 400° and line a medium baking sheet with parchment paper.

Season mozzarella sticks with salt and pepper, then dredge in flour.

Next, dip tenders in egg, and then in Cheetos crumbs.

Place mozzarella sticks on baking sheet and bake 25 minutes.

Serve hot, with ranch dressing for dipping.

# FRAN FRIES

**Made with love by Chef V**

## INGREDIENTS

### For Cheese Sauce

- 1 tablespoon canola oil
- 1/2 onion, peeled and sliced 1/2 inch thick
- 6 thin slices jalapeño
- 2 teaspoons whole black peppercorns
- 1/2 teaspoon kosher salt
- 1 tablespoon white wine vinegar
- 2 teaspoons white wine
- 2 cups heavy cream
- 2 cups grated American cheese
- 2 cups grated cheddar cheese

### For Fries

- 2 pounds Russet potatoes
- Canola oil for deep-frying
- Kosher salt

## INSTRUCTIONS

### For Cheese Sauce

Heat the oil in a large saucepan over medium heat.

Add the onions, jalapeños, peppercorns, and salt, and cook, stirring often, until the onions are translucent, about 5 minutes.

Add the vinegar and wine, and cook until liquid has almost completely evaporated, about 5 minutes. Stir in the cream. Remove the pan from the heat and let the cream steep for 30 minutes to build flavor.

Return the saucepan to the stove and heat over medium until very warm (don't let it come to a boil).

Meanwhile, put the American and cheddar cheeses into a large heatproof bowl. Pour the hot cream through a strainer (to remove the solids) over the cheeses, stirring until the cheese melts and the sauce is smooth, about 3 minutes.

Sauce will keep, if covered and refrigerated, for up to 1 week. You can easily reheat the sauce in a microwave or over a pot of gently simmering hot water.

# FRAN FRIES (CONTINUED)

(Above) Slicing of potatoes into desired size for fries.

(Above) Pouring hot cream through a strainer (to remove the solids) over the cheeses.

(Above) Stirring the hot cream until the cheese melts and the sauce is smooth.

## Preparation

Cut the potatoes into sticks about 1/4-inch thick around. As you cut the potatoes, place them into a large bowl of ice water to prevent them from browning (this also helps to release some of the starch).

Once you've cut all your potatoes, rinse them under cold water until the water runs clear.

Place the potatoes on paper towel-lined sheet trays and dry them thoroughly.

Heat 3-inches of oil in a large saucepan until a deep-fry thermometer reaches 320°F. Working in batches, fry the potatoes until cooked through, but still slightly raw in the center, about 2 minutes.

Using a slotted spoon, transfer the fries to a paper towel-lined baking sheet. Repeat with the remaining potatoes, then refrigerate the fries for at least 15 minutes before frying them again.

Increase the temperature of the oil to 375°F. Working in batches, cook the fries until golden and crispy, about 1 1/2 minutes, stirring constantly to keep them moving and cooking evenly.

Transfer to a paper towel-lined baking sheet and season with salt.

Wrap a bunch of fries with bacon and serve with cheese sauce, ketchup, or whatever your little heart desires.

### Be Strong After School Club Secret:

The Fran Fries are the result of a student suggestion. Seventh grader Franteria asked Chef Vanessa to show the students how to make bacon wrapped cheese fries. Chef Vanessa not only fulfilled Franteria's request, but she also named the dish after the student because they came out so delicious. Thus, "Fran Fries" were born!

# VEGGIE DISHES

# EGGPLANT PARMESAN

**Made with love by Ms. Vasti**

## INGREDIENTS

- 2 1/4 pounds (about 2 large) eggplants
- 1 tablespoon kosher salt
- 1 tablespoon extra-virgin olive oil
- 2 cloves minced garlic (about 2 teaspoons)
- 2 28-oz cans of whole peeled tomatoes (preferably San Marzano) that have been diced, reserving the juices, or crushed tomatoes
- 1/2 cup finely chopped fresh basil
- Freshly ground black pepper
- 2 cups breadcrumbs
- 1 1/4 cups shredded Parmesan cheese, divided
- 1 cup all-purpose flour
- 4 large eggs, beaten (more if needed)
- 1/4 cup extra virgin olive oil (plus more to oil the sheet pans)
- 1 1/2 pounds fresh mozzarella, sliced into 1/4-inch slices

## INSTRUCTIONS

### For the Eggplant

Slice the eggplants into 1/4-inch to 1/2-inch thick rounds.

Combine 1 1/2 cups of breadcrumbs with 1/4 cup grated Parmesan cheese, and place in a shallow bowl or rimmed dish.

Set up your station so that you have flour in one shallow bowl, beaten eggs in another bowl, and the breadcrumb cheese mixture in another, in that order.

Working one at a time, dredge the eggplant slices first in the flour, then dip in the beaten eggs, and then dredge in the breadcrumb Parmesan cheese mixture.

Place on oiled sheet pan. Drizzle a little oil over the top of each breaded eggplant round.

Place breaded prepared eggplant slices in the oven. Cook for 18 to 20 minutes at 425°F, turning the slices over at the half-way point, until they are nicely browned.

Remove from oven, and let it cool to touch.

## For the Sauce

Heat 1 tablespoon olive oil in a 4-quart saucepan on medium heat. Add the minced garlic and gently cook for 1 minute or until fragrant.

Add the tomatoes and their juices, breaking up the tomatoes as you add them to the pot.

Increase heat to bring to a simmer. Then lower heat to maintain a very low simmer for 15 minutes, uncovered.

Add salt and pepper to taste.

Add the minced basil and remove from heat.

## Preparation

Preheat the oven to 400 degrees F.

Spread 1 cup of the tomato sauce over the bottom of a 9x13-inch casserole dish. Place a third of the eggplant rounds in a single layer covering the sauce on the bottom of the pan.

Layer half of the sliced mozzarella on top of the eggplant rounds. Sprinkle 1/3 cup of grated Parmesan cheese.

Place another third of the eggplant rounds over the cheese. Spread 1 cup of the sauce over the eggplant rounds. Layer the rest of the sliced mozzarella over the sauce. Sprinkle with 1/3 cup of grated Parmesan.

Bake until beginning to brown, about 30 minutes.

Serve immediately.

# J AND FAMILY'S EGGPLANT CURRY

Made with love by Joi, age 13

## INGREDIENTS

- 1/2 carrot
- 1/2 medium onion
- 3 garlic cloves
- Turmeric
- 1/2 eggplant
- Red curry paste (Pictured: 1 jar of Maya Kaimal Kashmiri Curry Indian Simmer Sauce)
- Oil
- Salt
- Pepper

## INSTRUCTIONS

Cut up the eggplant into thin slices and set aside for later.

Dice 1/2 an onion and 1/2 a cup worth of carrots into small pieces.

Add the onions and carrots into a large frying pan with oil and garlic

Add red curry paste into the frying pan.

Add the eggplant slices into the frying pan.

Once the eggplant is soft, you can add salt, pepper, and turmeric to your taste.

Stir and taste your food. If you are satisfied, you can plate your food.

# PASTA DISHES

# SUN-DRIED TOMATO PASTA

**Made with love by Chef V**

## INGREDIENTS

- 3 garlic cloves
- 4 ounce sun-dried tomatoes
- Olive oil
- Salt
- Paprika
- Basil
- 1 cup of half-and-half (or 1/2 cup heavy cream + 1/2 cup milk)
- 1 cup mozzarella cheese, shredded
- 1/4 teaspoon red pepper flakes

## INSTRUCTIONS

In a large skillet, cook 3 cloves of minced garlic and 4 oz of chopped sun-dried tomatoes in 1 tablespoon of olive oil on high-medium heat for about 1 minute.

Add 1 cup of half-and-half (or 1/2 cup of heavy cream + 1/2 cup of milk ) to the same skillet and bring to a boil. Then reduce to simmer.

Add 1 cup of shredded mozzarella cheese.

Simmer and stir until the cheese melts and forms a creamy pasta sauce.

Add 1 tablespoon of dried basil, paprika, and at least 1/4 teaspoon of red pepper flakes. Stir to combine.

Add your favorite cooked pasta, then enjoy!

# LOBSTER MAC & CHEESE

**Made with love by Chef V**

## INGREDIENTS

### For the Lobster

- 5 lobster tails (6 tails, if you want it meaty)
- 10 tablespoon unsalted butter divided
- 1 1/2 teaspoon Cajun seasoning

### For the Pasta

- 8 cups water
- 1 lb. cavatappi pasta

### For the Cheese Sauce

- 1 1/2 cup shredded mild cheddar
- 1 1/2 cup shredded Monterey Jack
- 1 1/2 cup shredded Gruyére
- 2/3 cup shredded Parmesan cheese
- 1 teaspoon olive oil
- 2 teaspoon minced garlic
- 1/2 cup all purpose flour
- 2 1/4 cup heavy cream
- 2 1/4 cup whole milk
- 1 1/2 teaspoon onion powder
- 1 1/4 teaspoon garlic powder
- 1/2 teaspoon dry mustard
- 1/2 teaspoon paprika
- 1/4 teaspoon cayenne powder

### For Preparation

- 2 large eggs beaten
- 1/2 cup panko crumbs
- Chopped parsley for garnish

## INSTRUCTIONS

### For the Lobster

Cut lobster tails in half vertically.

Roughly chop the lobster into large chunks in a medium pan and add butter and Cajun season. Cook on medium-low for about 6 minutes.

Set the lobster aside, while preheating the oven to 375 degrees.

### For the Pasta

Add water in a large pot along with some salt and boil pasta according to the package. Drain and set aside.

### For the Cheese Sauce

Toss all shredded cheeses together in a large bowl and set aside.

Add olive oil to pan and heat over medium-high heat.

(Above) Chef V adds and mixes half of the lobster into pasta.

(Above) Chef V sprinkles remaining shredded cheese over the lobster pieces.

Add garlic and cook for 1 minute then add 3 more tablespoons of butter to the pan and allow it to melt down.

Quickly whisk in flour and cook for approximately 1 minute.

Pour in heavy cream and whole milk continuing to whisk.

Season with salt and pepper to taste.

Stir in half of shredded cheeses and allow them to melt continuing to stir.

## Preparation

Once cheese melts down, turn off heat and set aside.

Add beaten eggs and 1 tablespoon of butter to pasta. Then stir together until butter has melted.

Add pasta to 9x13 inch baking sheet.

Next, pour and mix in as much of the cheese sauce as you would like (for super cheesy, use it all).

Add and mix in half of the lobster to the pasta.

Spread the remaining lobster over the mac and cheese.

Sprinkle the remaining shredded cheeses over the lobster pieces, leaving some of them bare so they will be seen once baked. (If you want this dish super cheesy, add extra shredded cheese.)

Finally, melt the remaining 2 tablespoons of butter in a small bowl and add breadcrumbs. Toss the bread crumbs and butter together, and then sprinkle the breadcrumbs over the top of the pasta.

Place the pan of pasta in the preheated oven for 27-35 minutes.

Once the bake time is complete, remove the pan from the oven and let it rest for 10 minutes before serving.

If desired, you can sprinkle parsley on top of the finished Lobster Mac & Cheese.

# CHICKEN LO MEIN

**Made with love by Chef V**

## INGREDIENTS

- 2 to 3 cups egg noodles
- 3 tablespoons vegetable oil
- 4 teaspoons ginger
- 2 teaspoons garlic
- 1/2 pound chicken breast sliced thin
- 1/2 carrot, shredded
- 1/4 pound baby bok choy
- 3 scallions, chopped

### For Sauce

- 1/4 cup of chicken stock
- 3 tablespoons oyster sauce
- 1 tablespoon soy sauce
- 1 teaspoon cornstarch
- 1 teaspoon sesame oil

## INSTRUCTIONS

### For Sauce

Stir together the chicken stock, oyster sauce, soy sauce, cornstarch and sesame oil. Then set mixture aside.

### Preparation

Heat a pan to high and add the vegetable oil. Once you see wisps of white smoke, add the ginger and garlic. Continue cooking until it turns light brown and fragrant (about 20 seconds).

Stir in the chicken and cook on medium heat for about 1 minute.

Add in the cooked noodles, carrots and bok choy to the pan and cook until tender (about 1 minute.)

Take the sauce that you previously set aside, pour and stir it into the pan.

Continue to cook until the chicken is cooked through and the sauce starts to bubble and thicken.

Transfer to a serving platter, garnish with the scallions and serve immediately.

# DESSERTS
# & DRINKS

# MARSHMALLOW AND PRETZEL BROWNIES

**Made with love by Ms. Jasmine**

(Above) Mixing 1/3 cup of marshmallows into brownie mix.

(Above) After baking brownie mix for 26-31 minutes.

(Above) Adding the remaining marshmallows and crushed pretzels to top of brownies.

## INGREDIENTS

### For Brownies

- 1 box of Betty Crocker Delights Supreme Triple Chunk Brownie Mix
- 1/4 cup of milk ( or water, if you prefer)
- 1/2 cup of vegetable oil

### For Additional Toppings

- 1 bag of mini marshmallows
- 1/4 cup of crushed pretzels
- Whipped cream

## INSTRUCTIONS

### For Brownies

Preheat the oven to 350 degrees.

Grease the bottom of a 11" x 7" pan.

Stir the brownie mix, milk (or water), oil and egg into a medium bowl until well blended.

Add 1/3 cup of marshmallows into brownie mix.

Spread the completed brownie mix into baking pan.

Bake for 26-31 minutes, or until you can insert a toothpick 2 inches from the side of pan and the toothpick comes out clean.

### For Additional Toppings

Add the remaining 1 cup of marshmallows to the top of your brownie. Then sprinkle the crushed pretzel pieces on top of marshmallows.

Place in oven for about 3 minutes or until marshmallows start to soften and melt.

Remove from oven and allow the pan to cool off. Cut your desired amount of brownie and serve with whip cream on the side.

# ARLENE'S MANDARINS DELIGHT

**Made with love by Ms. Grant, Teacher**

## INGREDIENTS

- 2 Dole Mandarins Fruit Gel Cups (Note: You can use any brand of mandarin fruit gel cups)
- A cup of yogurt in your preferred flavor (Pictured: Vanilla yogurt)
- Cool Whip or Whip Cream (optional)
- Granola (optional)

## INSTRUCTIONS

Place 1 Dole Mandarin Fruit Cup at the bottom of your cup. Then pour half a cup of yogurt into the cup.

Pour the second Mandarin Fruit Cup on top of the first layer of yogurt.

Pour another half a cup of yogurt into the cup. Do not stir.

Add granola on top of the yogurt to your taste.

Add a scope of Cool Whip (or any whipped cream brand) on top.

# HOT CHOCOLATE

## Made with love by Chef V

## INGREDIENTS

- 1 cup whole milk, divided*
- 1 cup heavy whipping cream
- 4 tablespoons granulated sugar
- 1 1/2 teaspoons cornstarch (reduce to 3/4 teaspoon if a thinner consistency is preferred)
- 4 1/2 ounces dark chocolate, callets or finely chopped pieces from a chocolate bar
- Whipped cream, optional for garnish
- Chocolate shavings, optional for garnish

## INSTRUCTIONS

In a medium, heavy bottomed saucepan over medium-high heat, whisk together 3/4 cup of the milk, cream and sugar. Heat, whisking occasionally, until the mixture starts to bubble around the edges.

Meanwhile, in a small bowl or liquid measuring cup with a spout, whisk together the remaining 1/4 cup milk and cornstarch until well combined. As soon as the milk mixture bubbles around the edges, add in the milk and cornstarch mixture and whisk until heated through, about 1 minute.

Reduce heat to medium-low. Then add in the chocolate and whisk until completely dissolved into the milk mixture and is thick enough to coat a spoon (about 5 minutes).

Remove from heat and pour into mugs. While this recipe fills 2 average-sized mugs, keep in mind that it's super rich, so you might want to consider serving 4 half full cups instead.

Garnish with a dollop of whipped cream and top with chocolate shavings if desired.

Serve immediately, as the drink will continue to thicken as it cools.

*partially used in more than one step

# S'MORES MILKSHAKE

**Made with love by Chef V**

## INGREDIENTS

- 22 Kraft Jet Puffed Marshmallows
- 5 Honey Maid Graham Cracker Squares
- 2 Hershey's Milk Chocolate Bars
- 10 scoops vanilla ice cream
- 2 tablespoons milk
- Additional Hershey's Milk Chocolate Bars and Honey Maid Graham Cracker Squares, for garnish

## INSTRUCTIONS

Place the marshmallows on a foil-lined baking sheet, and place under the broiler. Broil until toasted. Watch them closely, as this happens quickly, in about 1-2 minutes. Once toasted, set the baking sheet aside.

Place 5 graham cracker squares in a plastic bag and crush until finely ground. Pour the crumbs onto a small plate.

Break up 2 chocolate bars, and place in a bowl. Microwave for 30 seconds, stir, then microwave for about 30 seconds more, until melted. Dip the top of your glasses into the melted chocolate, then into the crushed graham cracker crumbs. Set aside.

Place ice cream and milk in a blender, top with 18 toasted marshmallows. Blend until smooth. If you have to add more milk, you can do so. The residual heat from the toasted marshmallows will help the ice cream soften.

Pour into glasses, drizzle with some of the remaining melted chocolate, top with remaining toasted marshmallows, and garnish with remaining graham cracker crumbs. If desired, you can also garnish with whole pieces of chocolate bars and graham crackers.